COMOROS

MADAGASCAR

KU-251-983

INDIAN OCEAN

500km

Capital cities
Provisional provincial capitals
Main towns

Pemba

Nampula

Quelimane

Lichinga

MOZAMBIQUE

Inhambane

MALAWI

Beira

Tete

Sena

Chimoio

Mutare

Xai-Xai

Maputo

Harare

Kadoma

Bulawayo

ZIMBABWE

× GREAT ZIMBABWE

Nelspruit

Mbabane

SWAZILAND

KWAZULU/ NATAL

Durban

Pietermaritzburg

NORTHERN TRANSVAAL

Pietersburg/ Lebowakgomo

EASTERN TRANSVAAL

Pretoria

PWV

Mmabatho

Johannesburg

Soweto

Sasolburg

LESOTHO

ZAMBIA

Hwange

Francistown

Serowe

NORTH-WEST

ORANGE FREE STATE

Maseru

East London

Bisho/
King William's Town

Molepolole

Gaborone

Kanye

Kimberley

Bloemfontein

EASTERN CAPE

Maun

BOTSWANA

Ghanzi

Tshabong

NORTHERN CAPE

SOUTH AFRICA

Port Elizabeth

NAMIBIA

Windhoek

Rössing

Walvis Bay

Lüderitz

WESTERN CAPE

Swakopmund

ANGOLA

Cape Town

SOUTH ATLANTIC OCEAN

20°

Tropic of Capricorn

Shown are South Africa's new provinces. See Rule and Law (page 28).

Mozambique

Botswana

Lesotho

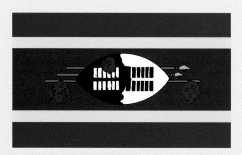

Swaziland

Namibia

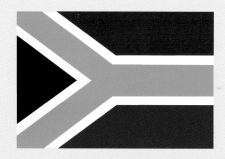

South Africa

Zimbabwe

WORLD FACT FILES

Southern Africa

Nick Middleton

SIMON & SCHUSTER
YOUNG BOOKS

First published in 1994 by Simon & Schuster Young Books
© Simon & Schuster Young Books 1994

Simon & Schuster Young Books
Campus 400
Maylands Avenue
Hemel Hempstead
Herts HP2 7EZ

Design	Roger Kohn
Editor	Diana Russell
DTP editor	Helen Swansbourne
Picture research	Valerie Mulcahy
Illustration	János Márffy
Commissioning editor	Debbie Fox

We are grateful to the following for permission
to reproduce photographs:
Front Cover: Tony Stone Images *above* (Colin Prior), The
Image Bank (Eric L Wheater) *below*; Biotica Picture Library,
page 11, *below*; Alec Campbell, page 29; Compix, pages
10/11 (Marlise Pepperell), 25 *above* (Juliete Coombe), 25
below (Mark Both), 41 *below* (Clare Draffin), 45 (Orde Eliason);
De Beers Consolidated Mines Ltd, page 35; Robert Harding
Picture Library, pages 18 *above*, 21 *below*, 22 *right*, 36 (G M
Wilkins), 38/39; The Hutchison Library, pages 18 *below* (Sarah
Errington), 30/31, 40 (John Hatt); Images of Africa Photobank,
pages 12/13 (Johann Van Tonder) 42/43 (Richard du Toit);
Lonrho plc, page 33; Mike Main, page 16; Dr Nick Middleton,
page 19; Panos Pictures, pages 8, 15, 20 and 32 (David
Reed), 13 (Bradley Arden), 21 *above* (Peter Barker), 22 *left*
(Neil Cooper), 34 (Trygve Bølstad), 41 *above* (Ron Giling);
Rex Features, pages 27 (Thomas), 39 *above* (John Reardon);
Rex Features/ Sipa-Press, pages 23 *left* (Juhan Kuus), 26
(Mark Peters), 44 (Tony Savino); Frank Spooner Pictures,
pages 8/9 (Gamma/Guy Hobbs); TRIP, pages 14 (Dave
Saunders), 17 (Dr Richard Price), 23 *right* (Jody Turco), 28,
37 (Juliet Highet); Tropix, pages 24 (M Auckland), 31 *above*
(John Schmid).

The statistics given in this book are the most up to date
available at the time of going to press

Printed and bound in Hong Kong by Paramount Printing Group

A CIP catalogue record for this book is available from
the British Library

ISBN: 0 7500 1485 7

96 8/18 38

C
O
N
T
E
N
T
S

Words that are explained in the glossary are printed in
SMALL CAPITALS the first time they are mentioned in the text.

INTRODUCTION

The region at the southern tip of the African continent is made up of seven countries: Botswana, Lesotho, Mozambique, Namibia, South Africa, Swaziland and Zimbabwe. If you ask anyone for their impressions of southern Africa, some might mention the abundant wildlife that can be seen in the region's wide open spaces. Others might mention deserts, because both the Namib and the Kalahari Deserts are in this area. Many people will talk about severe social problems. They will probably mention the unrest in South Africa which has been happening as its APARTHEID system is being

▼ **Great Zimbabwe was the largest city in the region when it was built more than 500 years ago.**

SOUTHERN AFRICA AT A GLANCE

● Population density: From 2 people per sq km in Namibia to 59 people per sq km in Lesotho
● Largest cities: Johannesburg/Soweto 2.0 million; Cape Town 1.9 million; Maputo 1.1 million, Durban 1.0 million, Pretoria 0.8 million, Harare 0.7 million
● Highest mountain: Thabana Ntlenyana (Lesotho), 3,482 metres
● Longest river: Zambezi, 2,650 kilometres
● Official languages: English in all countries except Mozambique, where it is Portuguese
● Major religions: Many African religions, Christianity
● Major resources: Diamonds, gold, platinum, uranium, chromium, coal, hydro-electricity
● Major products: Fruit, sugar-cane, tobacco, meat, timber, motor vehicles, clothing and textiles, chemicals, minerals
● Environmental problems: Soil erosion, DEFORESTATION, industrial pollution

◀ *Living conditions are poor and over-crowded for many in southern Africa today. This is Crossroads, near Cape Town, South Africa.*

dismantled. All of these impressions of the seven countries which make up southern Africa are accurate, but there is much more to tell.

The character of the whole region has been influenced for hundreds of years by European settlers who COLONIZED the countries. The Portuguese were the first to arrive, landing in Mozambique about 500 years ago. They gradually took control of eastern parts of the region from the powerful Muenemutapa Empire, which had risen after the decline of the Great Zimbabwe kingdom. The Portuguese were followed in other parts of the region by the Dutch and the English.

Conflicts between Europeans and black African groups lie behind many of the problems of southern Africa. Most of the countries have only been free of their colonial rulers for a short time. Mozambique became independent in 1975, Zimbabwe in 1980 and Namibia in 1990.

Southern Africa is a region of great contrasts. It includes some of Africa's richest countries (South Africa and Botswana) and some of the world's poorest nations (Lesotho and Mozambique). It contains deserts and fertile farmland, mountains and low-lying wetlands, small villages and large cities.

You can find out about all these aspects of the region in this book.

THE LANDSCAPE

The seven countries of southern Africa cover almost 3,900,000 square kilometres: two-fifths the size of the USA and 16 times the size of the United Kingdom. The region is bordered by the Atlantic Ocean to the west and the Indian Ocean to the east, and is crossed by the Tropic of Capricorn. Only three of the countries have coastlines – South Africa, Namibia and Mozambique.

Southern Africa's landscape varies from high mountains in the south, to sand desert in the west, grasslands in central areas and tropical forest in the north-east. Highlands known as the Great Karoo and the Drakensberg Mountains form a wide rim inland from South Africa's coastal plain. The highest parts of the Drakensberg range are

KEY FACTS
● From north to south, the region is about as long as it is wide: 2,700 kilometres from northern Namibia in the west to central Mozambique in the east.
● South Africa, the region's largest country, is 70 times the size of Swaziland, the smallest country.
● Areas of open country in southern Africa are known as "veld".

Pans in Botswana – are more than 150 kilometres across.

The northern parts of the region are covered in forests and woodlands. Mangrove trees, which can live in salt water, grow along much of the coastline of Mozambique.

At 2,650 kilometres, the Zambezi is southern Africa's longest river. It rises in Angola and forms most of the northern border of Zimbabwe before flowing through central Mozambique to the Indian Ocean. Dams which have been built on the Zambezi hold back the region's two largest lakes: Kariba on the Zimbabwe/Zambia border and Cahora Bassa in Mozambique. The Orange River (2,090 kilometres long), is the longest river that lies entirely within the region. It flows into the Atlantic Ocean.

▲*Much of the southern African landscape is desert. This view shows the Spitzkoppe hills in Namibia.*

▶*The Victoria Falls plunge 108 metres into the Zambezi. Their local name, "Mosi-oa-Toenja", means "Smoke that Thunders".*

over 2,000 metres. Most of Lesotho's territory, which includes the region's highest peak, Thabana Ntlenyana, is above this altitude.

The Namib Desert lies along the west coast of the region. Large parts of it are covered in sand dunes, more than 100 metres high. Sand covers much of the interior of the region too, although grass and small trees grow on the sandy soil. Salt lakes, which are dry for part of the year, are a common sight. These salt lakes are known as "pans", and the largest – Makgadikgadi

Southern Africa's climate can be divided into five main zones. The southern-most tip, South Africa's Cape, enjoys a Mediterranean climate, with cool, wet winters (May to August) and warm, dry summers (November to February). The slopes of the Drakensberg Mountains which face the most-frequent winds receive up to 1,500 mm of rainfall a year and the range's highest peaks are often capped by snow. This is a stark contrast to the western shores of Namibia, part of which is known as the "Skeleton Coast" as human and whale bones are frequently uncovered by the shifting sands – whaling used to be a big industry here and there were many shipwrecks. Annual average rainfall here can be as low as 15 mm. Moisture in this desert climate comes largely in the form of fog, a type of PRECIPITATION, which rolls in off the sea, cooled by the Benguela Current flowing from the Antarctic. This current keeps temperatures generally low compared with other desert regions, but 40°C has been reached at Swakopmund.

Much of the interior is distant from the sea and lies behind the Drakensberg Mountains. Here the climate is semi-arid to

KEY FACTS

● The worst drought in living memory hit most of southern Africa in 1991–93.
● Botswana's currency, Pula, means 'rain'.
● Zimbabwe is a tropical country. Lesotho and Swaziland lie outside the Tropics, while Botswana, Mozambique, Namibia and South Africa are crossed by the Tropic of Capricorn.

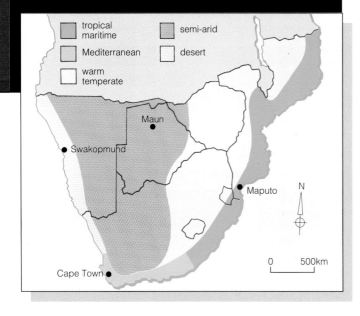

tropical maritime
Mediterranean
warm temperate
semi-arid
desert

Maun
Swakopmund
Maputo
Cape Town
N
0   500km

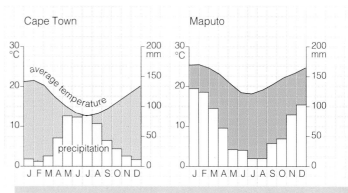

Cape Town

Maputo

average temperature

precipitation

J F M A M J J A S O N D   J F M A M J J A S O N D

the west and warm temperate in the east. Much of the western interior is called the Kalahari Desert. Most people think of deserts as having very little vegetation, but the Kalahari is covered in grass and low shrubs. Winters here are dry, with low humidity, clear skies and high temperatures. The annual average rainfall of less than 400 mm falls chiefly in the summer. The eastern interior is slightly wetter (up to 600 mm a year on average) and the low humidity and large number of sunshine hours make it a very pleasant and healthy climate for most of the year.

The eastern coastal region has a climate influenced by the sea, which is called a "tropical maritime climate". Rain falls throughout the year, but is heaviest in the summer months when average temperatures are 25–28°C and the air is humid. Winters are warm, but can be quite cold at the higher altitudes inland.

Many parts of the southern African interior suffer regular droughts, roughly every 18 years. In contrast, violent tropical storms called CYCLONES occasionally hit the eastern coastline, particularly in the north-east, between November and May.

◄ *Table Mountain provides a spectacular backdrop to the South African city of Cape Town. The climate here is like that in the Mediterranean.*

► *Much of southern Africa is regularly affected by drought.*

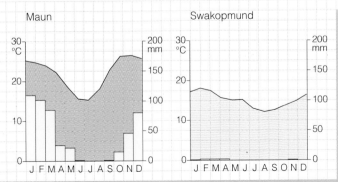

Maun

Swakopmund

◀Drilling for gold beneath the Witwatersrand, South Africa. The country is the world's largest producer of gold (see chart below), and gold is one of its major exports.

WORLD PRODUCTION OF GOLD, 1992 (tonnes)

South Africa 614 — 33.4%
USA 322 — 17.5%
Others 361 — 19.6%
Australia 240 — 13%
Canada 157 — 8.5%
Brazil 77 — 4.2%
Papua New Guinea 71 — 3.8%

Southern Africa contains some of the world's richest deposits of minerals. Iron, copper and gold have been worked for hundreds of years, and formed the basis of some powerful African trading kingdoms in the past.

Minerals are still very important to the economies of today's southern African countries. In 1886, the richest gold-bearing rocks in the world were discovered in South Africa, beneath a ridge known as the Witwatersrand. In just over 100 years, Johannesburg has developed from a gold-mining camp to become the region's largest city. Gold is still mined nearby, and the white heaps of rock waste from the mines rise like hills all around the city centre.

Since the discovery of gold, a wide range of other important minerals have been found and worked in South Africa. They include iron ore, copper, manganese, chrome, silver, nickel, phosphates,

▶ Thousands of tonnes of over-lying rock are stripped away by this machine to expose the coal beds at Hwange in Zimbabwe.

platinum, asbestos, tin, zinc and VANADIUM.

Of all the countries in the region, Botswana is the most heavily reliant upon minerals. In 1991, nearly 90% of its export income came from diamonds, copper and nickel. Botswana is also investing heavily in a new mineral development at Sowa Pan, part of Makgadikgadi, where a town and railway branch line are being built, to mine soda-ash, common salt and potash.

● South Africa has the world's largest known reserves of gold, platinum and chromium.

● Africa's largest reserves of coal are in South Africa.

● The Zulu name for Johannesburg, Egoli, means "City of Gold".

● In 1990, diamonds made up 40% of Botswana's GROSS DOMESTIC PRODUCT (GDP).

● Just 10% of the electricity generated by Mozambique's Cahora Bassa hydro-electricity scheme is enough to supply the whole country's current needs.

● Swaziland has one of the world's largest forests planted by people. It covers 103,566 hectares.

Namibia's economy too is dominated by the country's huge mineral wealth. Diamonds are particularly important, though there are vast reserves of copper, tin, lead, zinc and vanadium as well. Diamonds are also mined in Lesotho and Swaziland. Zimbabwe has the largest known platinum reserves outside South Africa.

Southern Africa's most important source of energy is coal. In Zimbabwe, the mines at Hwange in the north-west provide nearly 40% of the country's energy needs. Coal is also the most important commercial energy source in Botswana, South Africa and Swaziland. Some South African coal is converted into oil by a special process at Sasolburg, 80 kilometres south of Johannesburg. Mozambique too has extensive coal reserves and a large natural gas field which is yet to be exploited, while

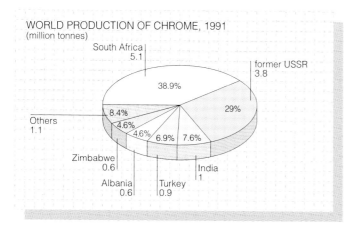

WORLD PRODUCTION OF CHROME, 1991
(million tonnes)

South Africa 5.1 — 38.9%
former USSR 3.8 — 29%
India 1 — 7.6%
Turkey 0.9 — 6.9%
Albania 0.6 — 4.6%
Zimbabwe 0.6 — 4.6%
Others 1.1 — 8.4%

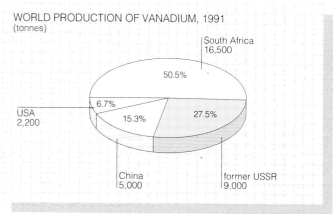

WORLD PRODUCTION OF VANADIUM, 1991
(tonnes)

South Africa 16,500 — 50.5%
former USSR 9,000 — 27.5%
China 5,000 — 15.3%
USA 2,200 — 6.7%

▲ *South Africa leads the world in the production of chrome and vanadium.*

◀ *By far the largest dam in the region is the one on the Zambezi at Cahora Bassa in north-western Mozambique. It is one of Africa's biggest hydro-electric schemes.*

Namibia's offshore gas fields represent a considerable source of future power supplies.

In many rural areas, however, wood is the main source of energy for cooking and domestic heating. In some heavily populated parts of the region fuelwood collection is a serious cause of forest loss. Other forms of energy, such as solar power and bagasse (a fuel made from sugar-cane residues), contribute little to the region's energy production.

Southern Africa also has a number of big rivers which have been harnessed to generate hydro-electricity. Several large dams, including the Hendrik Verwoerd and the P.K. le Roux, have been built along the part of the Orange River that flows through South Africa. They provide both electricity

and irrigation water for crop-growing land.

A new scheme, the Lesotho Highlands Water Project, is the largest water-supply scheme ever undertaken in Africa and will take 30 years to complete. It aims to provide extra water to the Johannesburg/ Pretoria area of South Africa and hydro-electricity to Lesotho.

Namibia has some of the world's largest deposits of uranium, although the country has no nuclear industry. The mine at Rössing, near the coast 200 kilometres west of Windhoek, is the largest open-cast uranium mine in the world. All of its uranium is exported. South Africa is the only southern African country which generates nuclear power.

It should not be forgotten that the landscapes and wildlife of southern Africa

▲ Tourists who visit the Okavango Delta in northern Botswana travel the wetlands in a traditional dug-out canoe called a MOKORO.

are also important natural resources. For example, in rural areas animals are hunted for their meat and plants are put to many different uses. In addition, wilderness areas which are protected in national parks and game reserves, attract tourists both from within the region and from all over the world. They come to marvel at the natural landscapes and their animals, and the money that tourism brings in is an increasingly important source of income for many countries in the region. For example, nearly 140,000 holiday-makers visited Botswana in 1990, compared with 84,000 in 1980.

POPULATION

The long history of people migrating to southern Africa has created a very diverse population. Today, the main population groups include a large number of African peoples, Europeans, Asians and a growing number of mixed-race people, known as COLOUREDS in South Africa and as MULATTOS in Mozambique.

In the past, in all the countries of the region, people of European descent ruled over large numbers of Africans, often employing oppressive measures to gain and maintain control. When South-West Africa – now called Namibia – was colonized by Germany in the 19th century, thousands of Herero and Nama peoples were massacred. During most of the 20th century, Africans in Mozambique were forced to work for very

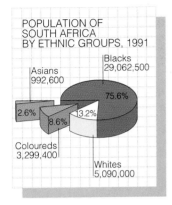

POPULATION OF
SOUTH AFRICA
BY ETHNIC GROUPS, 1991

Asians
992,600

Blacks
29,062,500

75.6%

2.6% 8.6% 13.2%

Coloureds
3,299,400

Whites
5,090,000

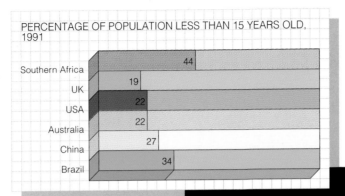

PERCENTAGE OF POPULATION LESS THAN 15 YEARS OLD,
1991

Southern Africa	44
UK	19
USA	22
Australia	22
China	27
Brazil	34

◀ *All the countries of southern Africa have very young population structures.*

▲ *Although black Africans are by far the largest group in South Africa, they include many different peoples.*

◀ *Long dresses introduced by missionaries in the 19th century have now become national dress for Herero women.*

◀ *Goods grown and made in a wide region outside Maputo are brought to Mozambique's capital for sale in the market.*

▼ *Many Mozambicans who fled their homes in the countryside during the civil war now live as traders on the streets in the towns and cities.*

KEY FACTS

● The population of Johannesburg is more than twice the entire population of Swaziland.
● In Mozambique, there is one doctor for every 50,000 people, compared with one for every 1,640 people in Zimbabwe and one for every 420 people in the USA.
● The population density of southern Africa is 18 people per sq km. The figure for Europe is 680 per sq km.
● Swaziland's population will reach 1 million by the year 2000: up 20% over 1990.

little pay on Portuguese agricultural plantations. In many countries, Europeans took the best land and pushed black Africans into smaller, less fertile areas. These practices have halted in the last 30 years. South Africa was the last country to stop the official discrimination between whites and blacks, with the ending of apartheid in the early 1990s.

DIFFERENT PEOPLES

Although outsiders often talk about black people and white people in southern Africa, the true make-up of the population is much more complex. In South Africa, more than 75% of the population consists of black Africans, but this group includes many different peoples. There is a small number of people who trace their roots back to the region's earliest inhabitants: the San or "Bushmen", the Khoikoi and the Bergdamara. Larger black African tribal groupings can be divided into the Nguni (who include the Zulu, Swazi, Ndebele, Pondo, Temba and Xhosa), the Sotho and the Tswana.

The white people in South Africa have very different origins too. The Afrikaners are descended from Dutch settlers who arrived from the 17th century onwards. There are also descendants of French, British and German colonists, as well as all sorts of Europeans who came to South Africa from other African countries.

South Africa is not the only country where different black African peoples have competed for power. In Zimbabwe the Shona people, who make up 80% of the black population, have competed with the Ndebele, who form the other 20%, since independence in 1980.

MIGRATIONS

Large-scale migration has continued in recent decades. Many male workers from neighbouring countries work in South Africa – in the mines, on farms and in factories. South Africa employs more than 50,000 workers from Botswana, about 25% of whom work in the mines, and no less than 38% of all Lesotho's adult male workers.

Migrations have also occurred for other reasons. The war in Mozambique led to about 1.5 million people leaving their country to live in refugee camps in countries such as Malawi and Zimbabwe. Another 4.5 million fled their villages to live in towns and cities which were more secure. Since the end of the fighting in 1992, many of these people

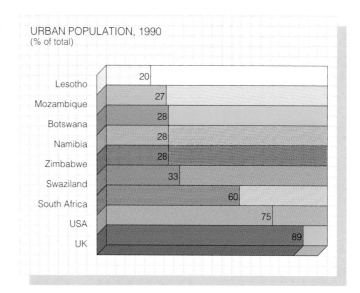

URBAN POPULATION, 1990
(% of total)

Lesotho	20
Mozambique	27
Botswana	28
Namibia	28
Zimbabwe	28
Swaziland	33
South Africa	60
USA	75
UK	89

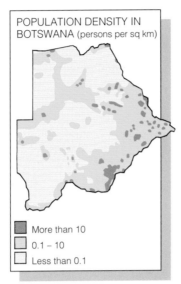

POPULATION DENSITY IN
BOTSWANA (persons per sq km)

■ More than 10
□ 0.1 – 10
□ Less than 0.1

have been returning to their homes. Some have been away for ten years or more.

YOUNG POPULATIONS

The population of southern Africa is growing fast. The proportion of young people is very high: about 44% in the region are below the age of 15. This compares with around 20% in countries such as the UK and the USA. As these young people grow up and have children, the size of the national populations will rise still faster. Governments in southern Africa are concerned about this rapid growth.

▲ *Harare, the capital of Zimbabwe, is a modern, rapidly growing city.*

◄ *Children in the region are very skilled at making their own toys.*

► *The San, or "Bushmen", were the earliest inhabitants of the Kalahari Desert. Traditionally they hunt animals and collect wild plants for their food.*

DAILY LIFE

FAMILY LIFE

Families in southern Africa are often large. It is quite common for children, parents, grandparents, cousins, uncles and aunts all to live together under one roof. In rural areas children help their parents in the fields or around the house – cleaning, collecting water, and looking after animals.

In many areas, particularly in cities, there is a wide gap between rich and poor. Richer families often have fewer children, live in large houses (perhaps with a swimming pool) and drive luxury cars. Most can afford to employ cooks, cleaners and nannies. Some of these domestic servants have their own accommodation in part of the main family house, while others travel every day to work in their employer's house and have to do their own housework at home each evening as well. Most of the servants are black, while their employers are richer people from many ethnic groups.

Many men from Lesotho and some from

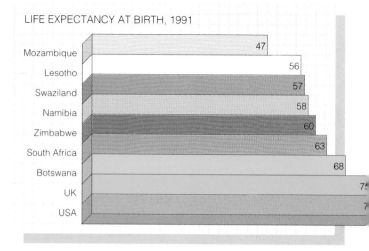

LIFE EXPECTANCY AT BIRTH, 1991

Mozambique	47
Lesotho	56
Swaziland	57
Namibia	58
Zimbabwe	60
South Africa	63
Botswana	68
UK	7?
USA	7?

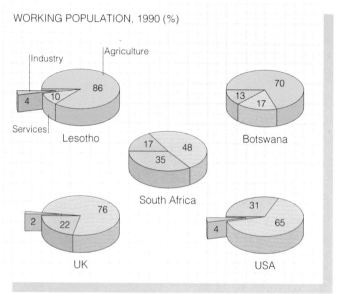

WORKING POPULATION, 1990 (%)

Industry / Agriculture / Services

Lesotho — 4, 10, 86
Botswana — 13, 17, 70
South Africa — 17, 48, 35
UK — 2, 22, 76
USA — 4, 31, 65

▼ *Collecting water is a daily chore for many people in rural southern Africa. This hand pump is in a village in southern Zimbabwe.*

▼ *Donkeys are used to carry the water home from a well in rural Lesotho.*

▲*Rugby is a very popular game, especially in South Africa. Soccer too is played throughout the region.*

▲*It is still common to see richer white people being waited on by a black servant, although today more black people are becoming prosperous.*

Botswana, Swaziland and Mozambique, live away from their families for many months at a time, because they work a long way from home in South Africa. For most of the year they live with other workers and send money home to their wives, who have to bring up the children without a husband. In Mozambique many families have also been broken up by the war. About a quarter of a million Mozambican children have become orphans, have been abandoned or have lost contact with their families.

EDUCATION
Primary school education is free in all the countries of southern Africa, although it is not compulsory in Botswana or Swaziland. Even so, not all children go to school. Some have to work for their living instead. Others lose out on education because there are no schools near them, particularly in country areas. In Mozambique many rural school buildings

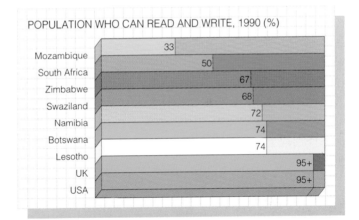

POPULATION WHO CAN READ AND WRITE, 1990 (%)

Country	%
Mozambique	33
South Africa	50
Zimbabwe	67
Swaziland	68
Namibia	72
Botswana	74
Lesotho	74
UK	95+
USA	95+

KEY FACTS

● Afrikaners are the only European group in Africa to have developed their own language, Afrikaans, which is based on Dutch.
● In Mozambique, 149 out of every 1,000 babies die before their first birthday. In Botswana, the figure is 36 per 1,000, while in the UK, it is 7 per 1,000.
● In Swaziland, 81% of children of primary school age go to school, compared with 4.5% in Mozambique.

DAILY LIFE

▶ *A Christian wedding in Botswana. The Gospel on the wall behind the priest is written in Setswana.*

▼ *Portuguese, Mozambique's official language, is included in "others" in this chart.*

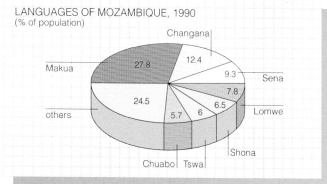

LANGUAGES OF MOZAMBIQUE, 1990
(% of population)

- Changana
- 12.4
- 9.3 Sena
- 7.8
- Makua 27.8
- others 24.5
- 6.5 Lomwe
- 5.7 6
- Shona
- Chuabo Tswa

were destroyed during the war.

Many schools are run by the state, but there are also private schools and those run by church groups. In Lesotho most education is provided by three Christian church missions – Evangelical, Roman Catholic and Anglican – under the direction of the Ministry of Education.

A large proportion of the adults in southern Africa cannot read or write. Botswana and Lesotho have the highest levels of literacy: 74%. In Mozambique, by contrast, just 33% of adults are literate. Although half of South Africa's population cannot read or write, the rate of illiteracy is much greater among the black population than among the whites.

English is the most widely spoken official language in southern Africa. In South Africa there are 10 secondary official languages, including Afrikaans, while in Lesotho the second official language is Sesotho and in Swaziland it is siSwati. Portuguese is the official language of Mozambique. Not everyone in these countries can speak the official language, however. In Mozambique, for example, less than a quarter of the population speaks Portuguese. Most Mozambicans speak one or more of the country's 16 main African languages.

RELIGION

Many different types of Christianity have been introduced to southern Africa by missionaries, and various Christian churches are found all over the region. Roman Catholicism is a major religion in Mozambique, and the Dutch Reformed church is dominant in parts of South Africa. About 50% of the population of Namibia are

▶ *Traditional dancing is enjoyed all over the region. African rhythms have influenced Western music too.*

Traditional doctors in Zimbabwe use medicines prepared from plant and animal matter. Nearly 70% of patients go to a traditional healer at some stage in their treatment.

members of the Lutheran church. Other religions include Islam, which is widely practised in northern coastal parts of Mozambique, while many of the peoples in the region who originated in the Indian sub-continent are Hindus. These imported

religions exist side by side with the traditional African worship of ancestors who inhabit a world of spirits. Many Africans who pray in church on a Sunday also consult the spirits of their ancestors on important matters in their daily lives.

People demonstrating for fair elections in the run-up to Namibia's independence from South African rule in 1990.

There are two monarchies in southern Africa: Lesotho and Swaziland. In Lesotho, the King acts through his Council of Ministers and is advised by a Military Council. The country is divided into 11 administrative districts, each with a District Secretary who co-ordinates government activity in the area, working with tribal chiefs. In Swaziland, all adults can vote in elections. Their elected representatives then decide who will sit in the two houses of Parliament, the Upper House and the House of Assembly.

Elections for Namibia's first nationally elected body, the National Assembly, took place in November 1989. The South West African People's Organization (SWAPO) won 41 of the 72 seats, with the Democratic Turnhalle Alliance winning 21. The National

Assembly's first task was to adopt the country's independent Constitution, which it did unanimously in 1990.

Botswana has a democratically elected National Assembly, with 34 members, which governs with the aid of a 15-member House of Chiefs. The Botswana Democratic Party is the most important political party.

In Zimbabwe, traditional chiefs take up ten seats in a single Parliament, the House of Assembly. All Zimbabweans over the age of 18 are eligible to elect 120 members of this 150-seat body. ZANU

(PF) is the dominant party in Zimbabwe.

For most of the time since independence, only one political party was allowed in Mozambique, the Frente de Libertação de Moçambique (Frelimo). But this changed in 1990. The country's other main party is the Resistência Nacional Moçambicana

INDEPENDENCE

COUNTRY	DATE	FORMER COLONIAL POWER	
Botswana	1966		Britain
Lesotho	1966		Britain .
Mozambique	1975		Portugal
Namibia	1990		South Africa
South Africa	1910		Britain
Swaziland	1967		Britain
Zimbabwe	1980		Britain

KEY FACTS

● In Swaziland, political parties are banned under the 1978 Constitution.
● So-called independent black "homelands" within South Africa, such as Transkei and Ciskei, were never recognized as separate countries by the outside world.
● Fighters from both Renamo and Frelimo are now being brought together to make up a new army in Mozambique.
● Botswana did not have an army until 1977, when the Botswana Defence Force was formed.
● Lesotho is the only country in the region with a military government. The government has been overthrown by military action 3 times: in 1970, 1986 and 1991.
● South Africa has 3 capital cities. Pretoria is the administrative capital (seat of government), Cape Town the legislative capital (where Parliament is) and Bloemfontein the judicial capital (seat of the Supreme Court).

◀ *The King of Swaziland, Mswati III, in a procession in front of his people on the day of his coronation.*

(Renamo), which fought against Frelimo in a bitter civil war that ended in 1992, when democratic elections were planned for October 1994.

South Africa has also been plagued by civil unrest. As the policy of apartheid began to be dismantled in the late 1980s, black political groups fought with each other and the largely white government. In 1990, the African National Congress (ANC), a black political party which had been banned for 30 years, was officially recognized along with several other previously unofficial political parties. The ANC and many other parties put up candidates for South Africa's first democratic elections in April 1994. Before that time, the large majority of South Africa's population had not been allowed to vote.

Many political groups were involved in setting down the guide-lines for a new, democratic Constitution in South Africa. The black HOMELANDS, set up under apartheid, were abolished and a new regional map of the country was drawn up. There are now nine regions in South Africa.

The new National Assembly is made up of 200 members elected on a national basis and 200 elected on a regional basis. Together with the Senate, these representatives will write a final Constitution for the country. The Cabinet, which will govern South Africa for five years, is composed of ministers nominated by parties that won at least 5% of the vote in 1994. The President, elected by the National Assembly, is a member of the party with the largest number of seats.

◀ *Social unrest, including violent demonstrations and murders, were widespread in South Africa as it moved towards democratic elections in 1994.*

▼ *People attending a "kgotla" at a town in Botswana. A "kgotla" is a public discussion where all can air their views on a wide range of issues.*

SOUTHERN AFRICA'S ARMED FORCES, 1992

Country	Number of personnel
Botswana	6,100
Lesotho	2,000
Mozambique	40,000
Namibia	7,400
South Africa	100,000
Swaziland	2,700
Zimbabwe	48,500

▶ *South Africa's new government structure came into being after the elections of April 1994. It will remain in place for 5 years, during which Parliament will draft the final Constitution.*

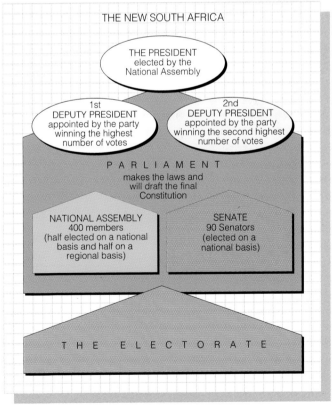

THE NEW SOUTH AFRICA

THE PRESIDENT
elected by the National Assembly

1st DEPUTY PRESIDENT
appointed by the party winning the highest number of votes

2nd DEPUTY PRESIDENT
appointed by the party winning the second highest number of votes

P A R L I A M E N T
makes the laws and will draft the final Constitution

NATIONAL ASSEMBLY
400 members
(half elected on a national basis and half on a regional basis)

SENATE
90 Senators
(elected on a national basis)

T H E   E L E C T O R A T E

FOOD AND FARMING

Most southern Africans work on the land, and the farming sector makes an important contribution to the economies of all the countries in the region. Many farmers produce enough food for their families, a way of life called SUBSISTENCE FARMING, but they sell any extra they may produce. Much of the work in the fields is done by hand, and the family may also keep a few animals.

Other forms of agricultural production occur on large plantations, with machines used for much of the ploughing, planting and harvesting. Irrigation equipment is used in drier areas. Many of the products grown in this way are exported, such as irrigated cotton from Mozambique and wine and fruit from the south-western Cape region of South Africa. Crops are important exports for several countries. Sugar-cane, for example, is Swaziland's largest crop and sugar makes up about a third of the country's exports by value. In Zimbabwe, tobacco brings in about 20% of all foreign exchange earnings.

The predominantly dry climate in Namibia and Botswana means that crop cultivation is difficult, so cattle-raising is the most important form of farming. In Botswana this is the chief industry after diamond mining. Livestock graze on almost 60% of the land

▼ *Grape harvesting in South Africa's south-western Cape region.*

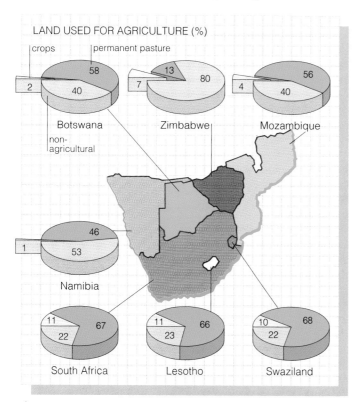

LAND USED FOR AGRICULTURE (%)

crops | permanent pasture

Botswana: 2, 58, 40
non-agricultural
Zimbabwe: 7, 13, 80
Mozambique: 4, 56, 40
Namibia: 1, 46, 53
South Africa: 11, 22, 67
Lesotho: 11, 23, 66
Swaziland: 10, 22, 68

▲ *Agriculture is a major form of land-use across the region. The dry climate in Botswana and Namibia limits opportunities for growing crops.*

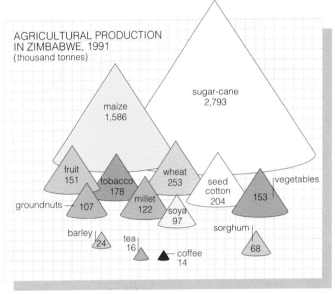

AGRICULTURAL PRODUCTION
IN ZIMBABWE, 1991
(thousand tonnes)

sugar-cane
2,793

maize
1,586

fruit
151

tobacco
178

wheat
253

seed
cotton
204

vegetables

153

groundnuts — 107

millet
122

soya
97

barley
24

tea
16

coffee
14

sorghum

68

◄*Hoeing the fields by hand is a very common sight in rural southern Africa. This woman is growing maize.*

area, and large quantities of beef are exported to the countries of the European Union. Botswana has some large ranches, but 80% of the 2.9 million cattle are owned by traditional farmers, mostly in small herds of less than 20 beasts. They provide meat and milk, transport, and labour for ploughs and carts.

The relatively small amount of land available for farming is a serious issue in many countries. In Lesotho, about 11% of the land is suitable for cultivation, and virtually all of this is already used. In the fertile western strip of the country there are about 200 people per square kilometre, compared with 59 per square kilometre for the country as a whole. Sheep, goats and cattle graze the more mountainous areas.

Population pressure is also great in certain parts of other countries, including Botswana, South Africa and Zimbabwe, but for different reasons. In 1990, 4,000 mostly white farmers owned 12 million hectares in

FOOD AND FARMING

▶ *Zebra and cattle graze side by side in this grassland area of Zimbabwe. The two animals eat different types of grass. This allows ranchers to produce more meat from the area than if the land was used to graze cattle alone.*

KEY FACTS

● About half of all families in Botswana own some cattle. There are more than twice as many cattle in the country as there are people.
● Swaziland's sugar industry is a major employer, providing 12,000 jobs in 1993.
● South African wines and brandies are exported to more than 25 countries, but 90% of production is consumed locally.
● South Africa produces 60% of southern Africa's fresh milk, 68% of its fruit, 70% of its eggs and 83% of its wool.

Zimbabwe, while 750,000 black peasants were crowded on to 15 million hectares of communal land. Since independence, the government has tried to re-distribute agricultural land more fairly. In 1992, a law was passed which allows it to force richer farmers to sell land at a fixed price, so that peasants can be settled there.

For those countries with a coastline, fishing is important both as a domestic food supply and for export. Namibia and South Africa have large commercial fishing fleets, each of which landed about 0.5 million tonnes of fish in 1991. Much of the fishing

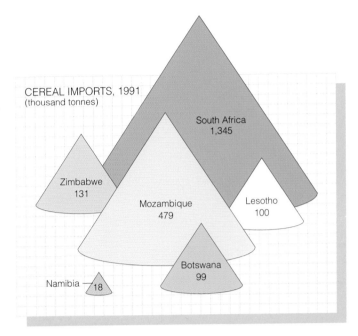

CEREAL IMPORTS, 1991
(thousand tonnes)

South Africa
1,345

Zimbabwe
131

Mozambique
479

Lesotho
100

Botswana
99

Namibia — 18

Mozambique it is CASSAVA, and in Lesotho and Zimbabwe it is maize. Most people mash up the husks and add water to make "mealie-meal", which looks rather like porridge. In towns and cities, however, fast food restaurants serve hamburgers and other convenience foods. Everybody in southern Africa enjoys eating outside, and luscious steaks are often the favourite item.

Drought is a hazard which regularly affects agriculture in southern Africa. Lack of rainfall reduces harvests and can lead to the death of livestock, either because of a shortage of grazing or a shortage of water. The worst drought in living memory hit large parts of the region in the early 1990s, when even normally self-sufficient countries such as South Africa and Zimbabwe had to import grain to feed their people.

from Mozambique is carried out by smaller boats. The country is famous for its large prawns.

The basic foodstuffs of southern Africa vary from country to country. In Botswana, sorghum is the principal food crop, in

◀ *Cotton cultivation was introduced to Mozambique by the Portuguese and cotton is still one of the country's leading crops. Irrigated fields produce very high yields per hectare.*

TRADE AND INDUSTRY

SOUTH AFRICA

South Africa is the most industrialized economy in the region and has a great influence on neighbouring countries. Its manufacturing industries have grown rapidly since the Second World War, especially the motor industry. South African cars, buses and other vehicles are exported to many parts of Africa. Other important manufacturing sectors include iron and steel, clothing and textiles, engineering and metal-working, chemicals, food, drinks and tobacco. For many years other African countries refused to trade officially with South Africa because of apartheid, but such trade continued unofficially. With the end of apartheid, many nations in Africa and beyond are again doing business openly with the country.

Despite the growth of manufacturing, the South African economy is still heavily reliant on the mining industry. Many

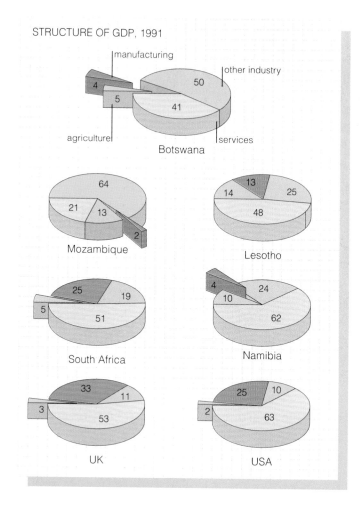

STRUCTURE OF GDP, 1991

▶ *The uranium processing plant at Rössing in Namibia. Uranium, the fuel used to produce nuclear energy, is one of Namibia's main exports.*

KEY FACTS

● Swaziland has a shortage of skilled labour to work in industry. Many of the better jobs are filled by foreign workers.
● Namibia received US $124 of aid per person in 1991, Botswana US $103 per person and Lesotho US $68 per person.
● All the southern African countries are members of the Southern African Development Community, a trading group set up in 1992 which includes Angola, Malawi, Tanzania and Zambia.
● The Southern African Customs Union, established in 1910, incorporates Botswana, Lesotho, Namibia, South Africa and Swaziland. Money paid in customs duties in these countries is shared among all the members.

▲ *Diamond sorting in Botswana. In 1992, southern Africa produced more than half of the world supply of rough diamonds.*

minerals, particularly gold, are exported. More than 0.5 million people were employed in South Africa's mines in 1992, the large majority of them in the gold mines. About 42% of these miners were migrant workers from neighbouring countries. Nearly a quarter were from Lesotho.

NAMIBIA, BOTSWANA AND ZIMBABWE

Exports of minerals also dominate the economies of Namibia and Botswana. When Namibia was ruled by South Africa, the mining and export of its minerals were banned under international law, although this continued anyway. Now such activity is legal, and profitable for Namibia. Most of Botswana's diamonds are exported to Switzerland, while the USA is the main market for its copper and nickel. These three products made up no less than 87% of Botswana's export income in 1991.

Gold is Zimbabwe's chief mineral product, but most of its exports are agricultural produce. Tobacco is the most significant. High-quality green coffee is also much in demand overseas, and one of the fastest growing areas is horticulture. Cut flowers, cultivated under carefully controlled conditions, are air-freighted to Europe in winter. For all Zimbabwe's exports, the United Kingdom is the most significant market, while South Africa provides the majority of its imports.

Zimbabwe also has a strong manufacturing sector, second only to that in South Africa. It is exceptional in Africa for its wide diversity of more than 6,500 products, making Zimbabwe self-sufficient in many areas and able to export to neighbouring African countries. Here, as elsewhere in Africa, the links between manufacturing and agriculture are strong. Manufacturing uses a significant proportion of Zimbabwe's agricultural production and agriculture in turn uses many inputs from local industries.

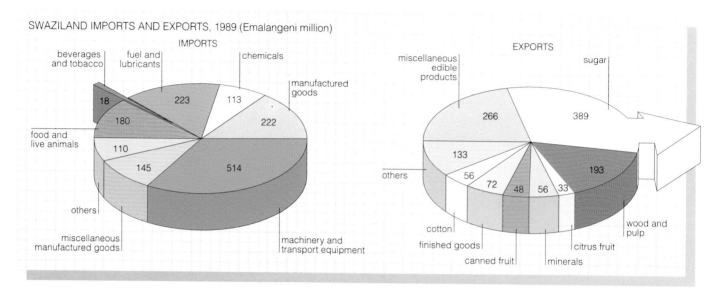

SWAZILAND IMPORTS AND EXPORTS, 1989 (Emalangeni million)

IMPORTS

beverages and tobacco — 18
fuel and lubricants — 223
chemicals — 113
manufactured goods — 222
machinery and transport equipment — 514
miscellaneous manufactured goods — 145
others — 110
food and live animals — 180

EXPORTS

miscellaneous edible products — 266
sugar — 389
wood and pulp — 193
citrus fruit — 33
minerals — 56
canned fruit — 48
finished goods — 72
cotton — 56
others — 133

LESOTHO, SWAZILAND AND MOZAMBIQUE

South Africa dominates the international trade of Lesotho and Swaziland. The exports from both countries are mainly PRIMARY PRODUCTS, and their imports chiefly consist of machinery, fuel, manufactured products and food. Lesotho's principal exports are wool, mohair and some diamonds. Swaziland's are sugar, which is processed from irrigated sugar-cane plantations in the east, fruits grown in the central region, and wood pulp from the forests of the rugged western mountains.

Mozambique is also very largely an agricultural country. Shellfish (mainly prawns), cashew nuts and cotton are its principal exports; Spain, the USA, Japan and South Africa are its main markets. Mozambique has the least developed manufacturing sector of all the southern African countries, and the factories that do

►Pottery produced at this workshop in Zimbabwe is sold to both visiting tourists and the domestic market.

exist suffer from outdated machinery and the devastation caused by nearly 30 years of war.

Mozambique is one of the least developed countries in the world. Its economy is very heavily reliant upon foreign aid, which contributed 69% of GROSS NATIONAL PRODUCT (GNP) in 1990, an extremely high proportion. Levels of aid to Mozambique have been rising since the mid-1980s, and in 1991 the country's national debt reached US $4,700 million. Repaying this debt is a virtually impossible task. Zimbabwe is the other southern African country which has run up a huge national debt. It stood at US$ 3,429 million in 1991.

◄The port at Durban in South Africa – one of the region's largest ports. The volume of trade carried on the railway lines between Durban and the Johannesburg/ Pretoria area make them among the busiest lines in Africa.

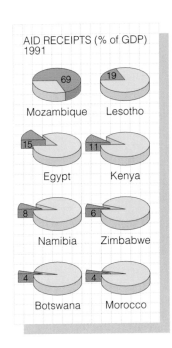

AID RECEIPTS (% of GDP) 1991

69 Mozambique
19 Lesotho
15 Egypt
11 Kenya
8 Namibia
6 Zimbabwe
4 Botswana
4 Morocco

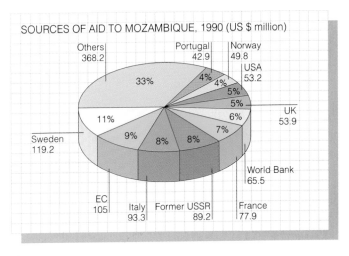

SOURCES OF AID TO MOZAMBIQUE, 1990 (US $ million)

Others 368.2 — 33%
Portugal 42.9 — 4%
Norway 49.8 — 4%
USA 53.2 — 5%
UK 53.9 — 5%
World Bank 65.5 — 6%
France 77.9 — 7%
Former USSR 89.2 — 8%
Italy 93.3 — 8%
EC 105 — 9%
Sweden 119.2 — 11%

▲Most of the major donors of aid to Mozambique are European countries.

TRANSPORT

The sheer size of many southern African countries means that transport is a significant problem. For farmers and those who work in rural industries, small private planes are a popular, although expensive, way of travelling in Botswana, Mozambique, Namibia, South Africa and Zimbabwe. These countries have dirt landing strips in many rural areas. Mozambique and South Africa also have comprehensive air transport systems between major towns and cities. Although Mozambique is a poor country, air transport was for a long time the only safe way of travelling during the war. All southern African countries have at least one international airport. Jan Smuts Airport in Johannesburg is the main international airport for the whole region.

Rail transport is important too, particularly for carrying freight. It is the principal way that the countries without coastlines import and export goods. Rail access to Mozambican ports is used by South Africa,

Swaziland, Botswana and Zimbabwe, as well as by Zambia and Malawi to the north. The fees Mozambique receives for the use of its railways and ports are an important source of income, and these facilities provide employment for significant numbers of people. Botswana is also looking towards Namibia's Atlantic Ocean ports for future trade routes; a trans-Kalahari rail link to the port at Walvis Bay should be completed by 1995.

Although the roads in and between the main towns and cities of southern Africa are

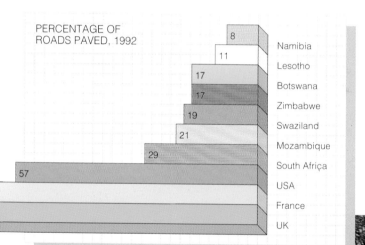

357,752 km

PERCENTAGE OF ROADS PAVED, 1992

8	Namibia
11	Lesotho
17	Botswana
17	Zimbabwe
19	Swaziland
21	Mozambique
29	South Africa
57	USA
92	France
100	UK

▶ *This gravel road in Namibia is typical of many all over southern Africa. Animals such as the donkeys in the picture are also widely used as a form of transport.*

21,244 km	USA
16,568 km	South Africa
	UK
3,131 km	Mozambique
2,745 km	Zimbabwe
2,382 km	Namibia
887 km	Botswana
301 km	Swaziland
2.6 km	Lesotho

LENGTH OF
RAILWAY TRACK, 1992

◄ *In most of southern Africa, trains are an important form of transport for people and freight. Major rail lines are being rebuilt in Mozambique following the end of the war there.*

paved, most roads in the region are dirt or gravel tracks. Four-wheel-drive cars are necessary along the roughest routes. Urban areas and many rural regions are served by buses and taxis which can be hailed at any point along their routes, but many rural residents rely upon their feet, bicycles or animal transport. Horses are a common

form of transport in the highland parts of Lesotho, for example.

In Botswana's Okavango Delta wetland, a traditional dug-out canoe known as a mokoro, which is made from a single tree trunk, is still widely used. A long pole is used to propel it.

THE ENVIRONMENT

nvironmental problems occur when people misuse natural resources. Southern Africa, like most parts of the world, faces many of these difficulties. Some of the most acute problems are a simple reflection of population pressure. Certain areas have high population densities and there are various reasons for this.

During the period when Namibia, South Africa and Zimbabwe were controlled by people from Europe, white rulers forced Africans to live in less fertile areas, where there was often over-crowding. When Germany governed Namibia, for example, cattle-herders were pushed into the northernmost strip of the country, known as Ovamboland. This region still suffers from over-grazing, which leads to loss of vegetation and soil erosion.

Similar over-use of soils and other natural resources has occurred in areas which South Africa called "homelands":

▲Elephant populations are severely threatened by poachers in some areas of Africa. But in parts of southern Africa their numbers have to be controlled by wildlife authorities.

zones of often poor soil over-worked by large, predominantly black, populations. In Zimbabwe, such areas were known as "native reserves". In both countries, these patterns of population distribution have left severe environmental problems.

Population density also varies widely in Lesotho. Large numbers of people cultivate the fertile western lowlands, while much fewer live in the mountainous areas. The country's rising population is over-using soils and erosion is a serious problem.

In Mozambique, the war forced many rural people to leave their fields for towns and cities where they would be safer. Large numbers of refugees crowding into

► *The collection of firewood is putting serious pressures on forests and woodland in some parts of southern Africa.*

POPULATION WITH ACCESS TO SAFE WATER, 1988–90 (%)

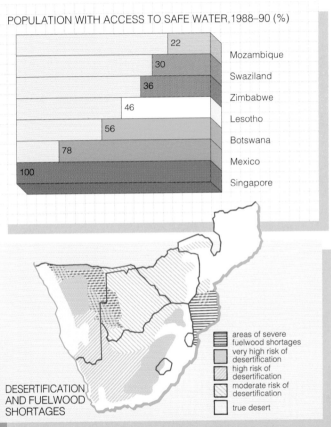

22	Mozambique
30	Swaziland
36	Zimbabwe
46	Lesotho
56	Botswana
78	Mexico
100	Singapore

DESERTIFICATION AND FUELWOOD SHORTAGES

- areas of severe fuelwood shortages
- very high risk of desertification
- high risk of desertification
- moderate risk of desertification
- true desert

▼ *Over-use of soils in Lesotho has caused some of the worst soil erosion in Africa.*

these areas devastated the surrounding woodland, which they chopped down for fuelwood. A shortage of farmland in safe areas has also meant that the soils in fields near towns and cities have been exhausted.

Other activities in Mozambique during the war years have also brought serious environmental problems. For instance, troops fighting the government killed large numbers of elephants to sell their ivory, using the cash to buy weapons. At independence in 1975, Mozambique's elephant population was about 65,000. Initial post-war estimates suggest that just 15,000 remain.

In contrast to Mozambique, and unlike the situation across most of Africa, the elephant population elsewhere in southern Africa is quite healthy. Elephant numbers in South Africa, Botswana and Zimbabwe are too great for the areas where they roam. So wildlife managers keep the numbers down by a process called "culling" – deliberate, planned killing to control animal populations.

Many southern African countries have a good number of national parks and other protected areas. South Africa's Kruger National Park, for example, covers an area of nearly 19,500 square kilometres. It protects 130 species of mammals, 114 of reptiles, 468 of birds and 48 of fish. These wildlife reserves are popular with tourists from many parts of the world, and the money they spend makes an important contribution to local economies.

The mining activities which are so important to several countries in the region have major environmental impacts. Gold, diamond and uranium mines scar the landscape and pollute waterways.

KEY FACTS

● There are more than 3,000 species of plant in Botswana. Most of these are used by rural people for food, medicines, fuel and building materials, and for making mats, ropes, nets and jewellery.

● Only about a fifth of Lesotho's population is served by sewage facilities.

● Zimbabwe's national plan for rural water supplies aims to provide clean water within 500 metres of every rural home.

● The Zambezi River has 340 known species of fish.

● There are about 24,000 species of flowering plant in South Africa – nearly 10% of all flowering plants on Earth.

● Mozambique's national parks and other protected areas were not protected at all during the war years.

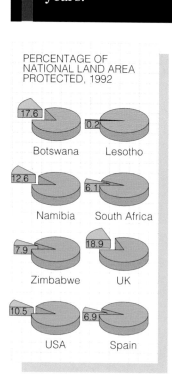

PERCENTAGE OF NATIONAL LAND AREA PROTECTED, 1992

17.6 Botswana
0.2 Lesotho
12.6 Namibia
6.1 South Africa
7.9 Zimbabwe
18.9 UK
10.5 USA
6.9 Spain

Industrial regions, such as the Witwatersrand in South Africa, produce serious air pollution from factories and coal-burning power stations.

Many large and growing urban areas lack adequate sewage systems and water supply. Most of the region's population have very limited access to water which is safe to drink. Collecting water is a time-consuming activity in rural areas. As the population is growing, this problem will become even greater for the governments of the region.

The need for careful management of environmental resources is recognized by the southern African governments. In Botswana, a National Conservation Strategy has been introduced in an effort to make sure that resources are used sensibly by cattle-herders, miners, business people and government alike.

▼ *Wildlife in their natural environment, such as here at Etosha Pan in northern Namibia, are an attraction for tourists.*

After a long history of being controlled by outside peoples, southern Africa can now look forward to a future where the majority of Africans can decide how to run their own affairs. The region as a whole has rich farmlands and huge mineral resources on which to build its future.

However, if the region is to develop, peace and stability are vital. Botswana, for example, has enjoyed a stable period of independence since 1966, but Mozambique has known independence without war only since 1992.

The development tasks faced by southern African governments, especially in rural areas, are huge. Basic needs such as clean water, sanitation and health-care are inadequate in many parts of the countryside. The standard of living in many of the poorer areas of the region's cities is also low.

Improving conditions for southern Africa's people is an ever-increasing task. The region has a young and rapidly growing population. Education is a key priority – and when people leave school, they want jobs.

With the ending of apartheid in South Africa, Africa's strongest economy, the region looks forward to more co-operation between all its countries.

▶ *Educating southern Africa's large young population is a priority.*

▼ *Nelson Mandela, South Africa's first democratically elected President. Peace and stability are essential for the region's future development.*

KEY FACTS

● In 1993, ANC leader Nelson Mandela and South African President de Klerk were jointly awarded the Nobel Peace Prize for their work in bringing democracy to South Africa.

● Mozambique's major task after the war is to help re-settle 5 million people driven from their homes.

● In 2000, the populations of Botswana and Swaziland are expected to be 40% higher than they were in 1990.

FURTHER INFORMATION

● BOTSWANA HIGH COMMISSION
6 Stratford Place, London W1N 9AE
Provides booklets, maps and information on
Botswana.

● LESOTHO HIGH COMMISSION
7 Chesham Place, London SW1 8NH
Provides maps and information on Lesotho.

● MOZAMBIQUE EMBASSY
21 Fitzroy Square, London W1P 5HJ
Provides an information pack on
Mozambique.

● NAMIBIA HIGH COMMISSION
6 Chandos Street, London W1
Provides information on Namibia.

● SWAZILAND HIGH COMMISSION
58 Pont Street, London SW1 0AE
Provides a map and information on
Swaziland.

● SOUTH AFRICAN EMBASSY
South Africa House, Trafalgar Square,
London WC2N 5DP
Provides booklets, maps and information on
South Africa.

● ZIMBABWE HIGH COMMISSION
Zimbabwe House, 429 Strand, London
WC2R 0SA
Provides maps and information on
Zimbabwe.

BOOKS ABOUT SOUTHERN AFRICA

Southern Africa, Judy Maxwell, Heinemann Children's Reference 1992 (age 11+)
Africa, Jocelyn Murray, Facts on File 1990 (age 10–12)
Zimbabwe: A Land Divided, Robin Palmer and Isobel Birch, Oxfam 1992 (age 11+)

Conflict in Southern Africa, Chris Smith, Wayland 1992 (age 13+)
Nelson Mandela, Richard Tames, Franklin Watts 1991 (age 8–11)

GLOSSARY

APARTHEID
Afrikaans word meaning separate development. The term was used of the South African government policy, before democratic elections, which discriminated against the non-white population.

CASSAVA
A food crop grown widely in tropical Africa, also known as "manioc".

COLONIZATION
A system where a country is occupied and ruled by people from a different country.

COLOUREDS
A term used of people of mixed black/white race, especially in South Africa.

CYCLONES
Tropical storms with very strong winds and heavy rain. In different parts of the world they are known as hurricanes, tornadoes or typhoons.

DEFORESTATION
The clearance of trees by people, either to burn them as fuelwood or to use the land for a different purpose, such as farming.

GROSS DOMESTIC PRODUCT (GDP)
A similar measure to GNP, except that GDP does not include money earned by a country from investments abroad.

GROSS NATIONAL PRODUCT (GNP)
The total value of all the goods and services produced by a country in a year.

HOMELANDS
Areas within South Africa during the time of apartheid where the government re-settled black people.

MOKORO (plural mekoro)
A dug-out canoe used in Botswana's Okavango Delta.

MULATTOS
A term used of people of mixed black/white race, especially in Mozambique.

PRECIPITATION
Rain, dew, fog, mist, frost, snow and hail are all types of precipitation.

PRIMARY PRODUCTS
Things produced which have not yet been processed by industry. They include all types of farm produce, and products of mining and forestry.

SUBSISTENCE FARMING
A form of livelihood in which someone produces only enough food for his or her family to eat.

VANADIUM
A soft, silver-grey metal used to make steel stronger.